THE REMARKABLE RONALD REAGAN

Cowboy and Commander in Chief

By Susan Allen

Illustrated by Leslie Harrington

Cataloging-in-Publication data on file with the Library of Congress
ISBN 978-1-62157-038-7

Published in the United States by
Regnery Kids
An imprint of Regnery Publishing, Inc.
One Massachusetts Avenue NW
Washington, DC 20001
www.Regnery.com

Manufactured in the United States of America

10 9 8 7 6 5 4 3 2 1

Books are available in quantity for promotional or premium use. Write to Director of Special
Sales, Regnery Publishing, Inc., One Massachusetts Avenue NW, Washington, DC 20001,
for information on discounts and terms, or call (202) 216-0600.

Distributed to the trade by
Perseus Distribution
250 West 57th Street
New York, NY 10107

Dedication

To my husband, George, whose partnership in everything has provided
a lifetime of adventures. And to our children—Tyler, Forrest,
and Brooke—who share the joy of reading and learning history
as they chart their own exciting courses.

Acknowledgments

It is with deep gratitude that I acknowledge the esteemed team
that worked diligently on this project. Michael Burgan, illustrator Leslie
Harrington, Diane Reeves, Cheryl Barnes, Marji Ross, and Regnery Kids
are all to be commended for their effort to help share the story of
the truly remarkable Ronald Reagan with all young readers who may
aspire to follow in the footsteps of one of America's
greatest presidents. Thank you all!

Do you ever wish you could grow up to be a football player or a movie star? Maybe you imagine yourself as governor of your state or even president of the United States. Do you ever dream of riding horses like a cowboy or cowgirl?

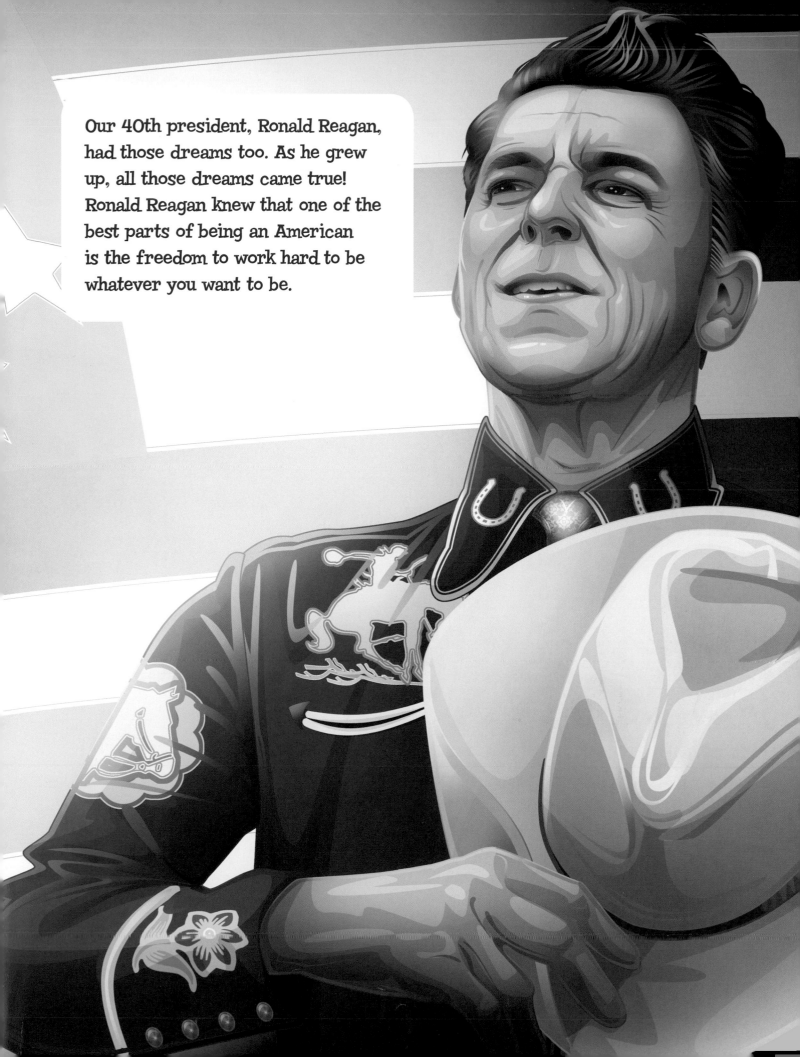

Our 40th president, Ronald Reagan, had those dreams too. As he grew up, all those dreams came true! Ronald Reagan knew that one of the best parts of being an American is the freedom to work hard to be whatever you want to be.

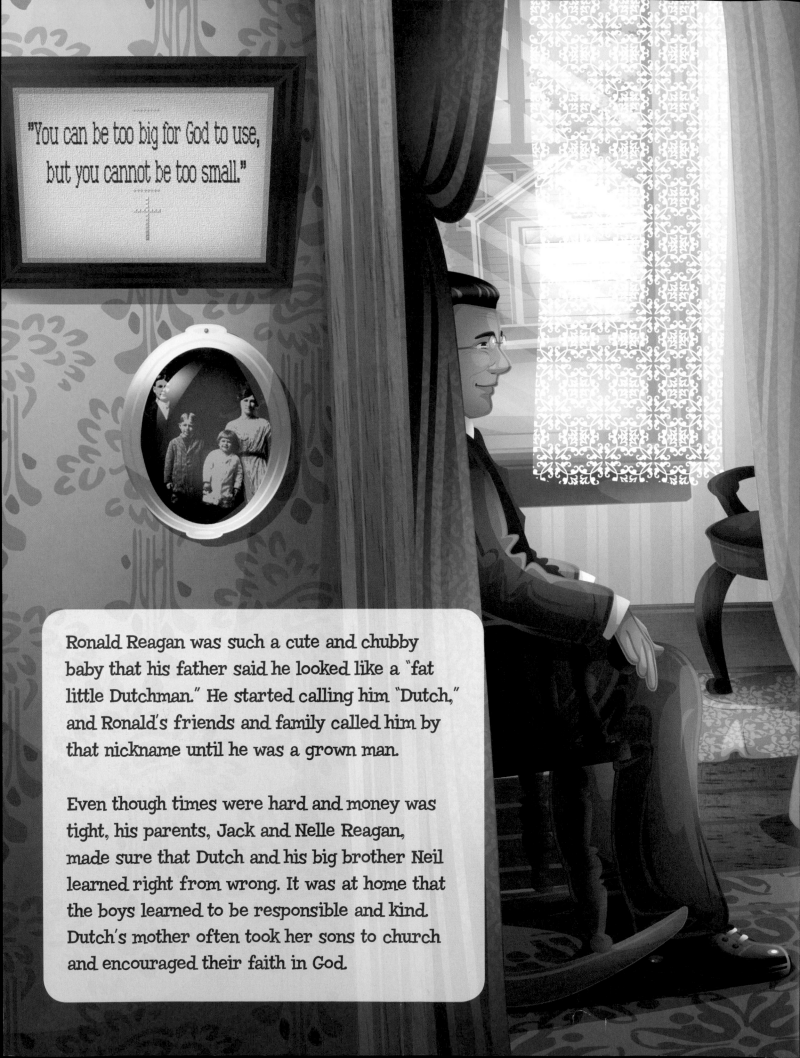

"You can be too big for God to use, but you cannot be too small."

Ronald Reagan was such a cute and chubby baby that his father said he looked like a "fat little Dutchman." He started calling him "Dutch," and Ronald's friends and family called him by that nickname until he was a grown man.

Even though times were hard and money was tight, his parents, Jack and Nelle Reagan, made sure that Dutch and his big brother Neil learned right from wrong. It was at home that the boys learned to be responsible and kind. Dutch's mother often took her sons to church and encouraged their faith in God.

Their father taught them to respect all people—no matter the color of their skin or how much money they had. Anyone needing a helping hand or a place to stay was always welcome in the Reagan home.

"Within the covers of the Bible are all the answers for all the problems men face."

Growing up, Dutch was always ready to try new things. He went out for
high school football and made the team. He ran track and played basketball.
He wasn't always the best player on the team, but he always tried his best.

Dutch loved to swim and spent seven summers working as a lifeguard.
He saved the money he earned to help pay for college. As a lifeguard
Dutch rescued seventy-seven people from drowning!

It was in high school that Dutch made his first appearances on stage—acting in school plays. He liked making the audience laugh and hearing their applause.

Dutch was only seventeen years old when he set off for Eureka College. There he kept busy with his studies, football, acting, and making speeches as student body president.

By the time Dutch graduated, he knew that he loved sports and was really good at public speaking. It was a dream come true when he got a job as a radio sports announcer.

Dutch often covered games being played many miles away from where his radio station was located. But his play-by-play calls were so enthusiastic no one knew he didn't have a front row seat at the game!

Baseball Today

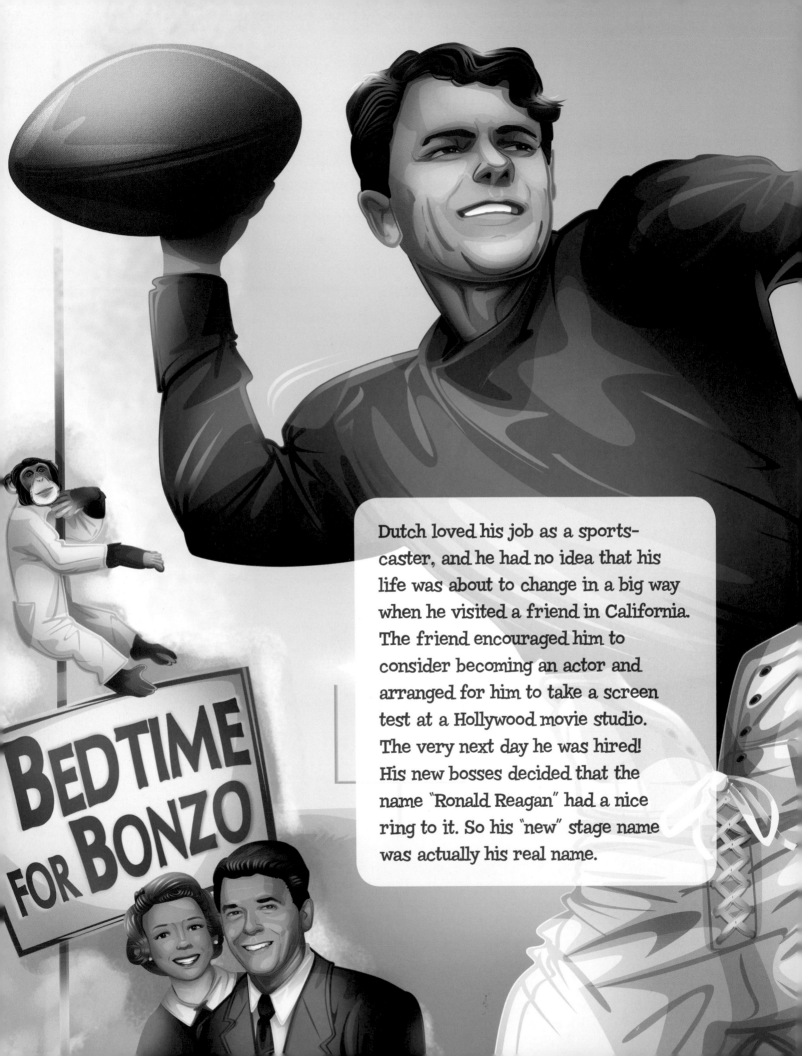

Dutch loved his job as a sports-caster, and he had no idea that his life was about to change in a big way when he visited a friend in California. The friend encouraged him to consider becoming an actor and arranged for him to take a screen test at a Hollywood movie studio. The very next day he was hired! His new bosses decided that the name "Ronald Reagan" had a nice ring to it. So his "new" stage name was actually his real name.

BEDTIME FOR BONZO

Just a few months later, he appeared in his first movie playing a radio announcer. One of his favorite roles was playing a real-life football star, George Gipp. In another movie, *Bedtime for Bonzo*, he co-starred with a chimpanzee! Ronald also found fame playing a cowboy in Old West movies. He loved riding horses so much that it sparked a new dream. He decided that one day he would own his own ranch so he could ride horses whenever he wanted.

COLOR BY **TECHNICOLOR**

Honolulu Star-Bulletin 1st EXTRA

PAGES -- HONOLULU - TERRITORY OF HAWAII U. S. A. SUNDAY, DECEMBER 7, 1941 — FIVE CENTS

WAR !

OAHU BOMBED B
JAPANESE P

(Associated Press by TransPacific Telephone)

SAN FRANCISCO, Dec. 7 P
ident Roosevelt announ
morning that Ja
attacked Pearl

SIX KNOWN DEAD, 21 MISSING

Attacks Made
On Defense Areas

Like millions of other Americans, Ronald's life took an unexpected turn on December 7, 1941. That was when Japanese planes bombed American ships at Pearl Harbor, Hawaii. America declared war and joined its allies to fight in World War II.

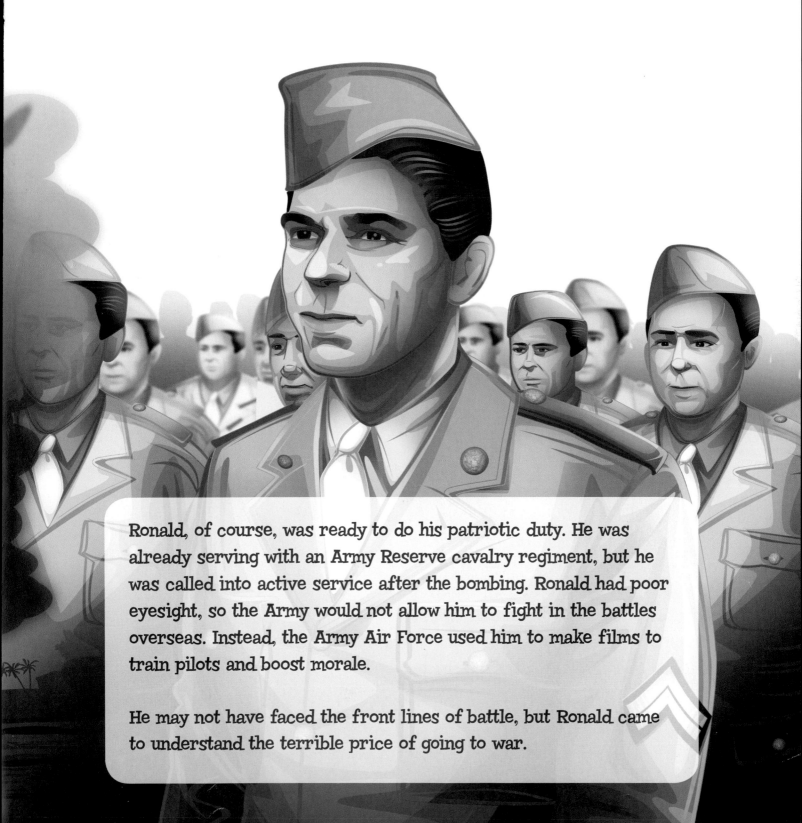

Ronald, of course, was ready to do his patriotic duty. He was already serving with an Army Reserve cavalry regiment, but he was called into active service after the bombing. Ronald had poor eyesight, so the Army would not allow him to fight in the battles overseas. Instead, the Army Air Force used him to make films to train pilots and boost morale.

He may not have faced the front lines of battle, but Ronald came to understand the terrible price of going to war.

During the war years Ronald married a talented actress named Jane Wyman. The young couple soon started a family—adopting a son named Michael and having a daughter named Maureen. A few years after the war ended, though, they divorced.

After the war, Ronald went back to making movies. During his acting career he made fifty-three movies. He was a star!

Family

He was so well-respected by other actors and actresses that they elected him president of the Screen Actors Guild. His job was to protect the rights of actors in matters of wages, health care, and safety.

Ronald met a beautiful actress named Nancy Davis. They fell in love, married, and had two children, Patti and Ron. The couple shared a long and happy marriage that lasted the rest of his life.

"You and I have a rendezvous with destiny."

Ronald strongly believed in democracy, in which people are free and have a say in their government. At that time, people in many places around the world did not have this same freedom. He started to speak out about this, and people started to listen. In 1964 he was invited to give a very important speech on national television. This was a huge turning point in Ronald's life.

Ronald had many friends who believed he could help his fellow citizens in California. They encouraged him to run for governor. Governor Reagan made tough choices that made his state a better place to live and work.

After Reagan's eight years as governor, he and Nancy bought a large ranch in the mountains outside Santa Barbara, California. They named it "Rancho del Cielo," which is Spanish for "Ranch in the Sky." The ranch was a place where Reagan could pull on his boots, put on a cowboy hat, and clear his mind with hard work and long horseback rides.

It was a beautiful place where he could unwind, enjoy private time with Nancy, and entertain family and friends. To Reagan it really was heaven on earth—and another one of his dreams come true.

As much as he enjoyed the ranch, Reagan knew he must do more to make America stronger. In 1976 he made a big decision—he would run for president of the United States! Reagan didn't win that race, but he tried again four years later. This time millions of Americans elected Ronald Reagan to be the 40th president of the United States.

In his inauguration speech he said, "We have every right to dream heroic dreams. Those who say that we are in a time when there are no heroes just don't know where to look."

Two months after he became president, Reagan gave a speech at a hotel in Washington, D.C. After the speech, he left the building, walking past a crowd of reporters toward a waiting limousine just thirty feet away. Suddenly six loud popping noises were heard. Someone was trying to shoot the president!

Within seconds, three people were hit. At first, no one realized Reagan had been shot. After Secret Service agents pushed him into the protection of his armored car, Reagan noticed a pain in his side. He thought it was a broken rib but later learned that the last shot had bounced off the door of the car and struck him under the arm. The bullet stopped just one inch from the president's heart!

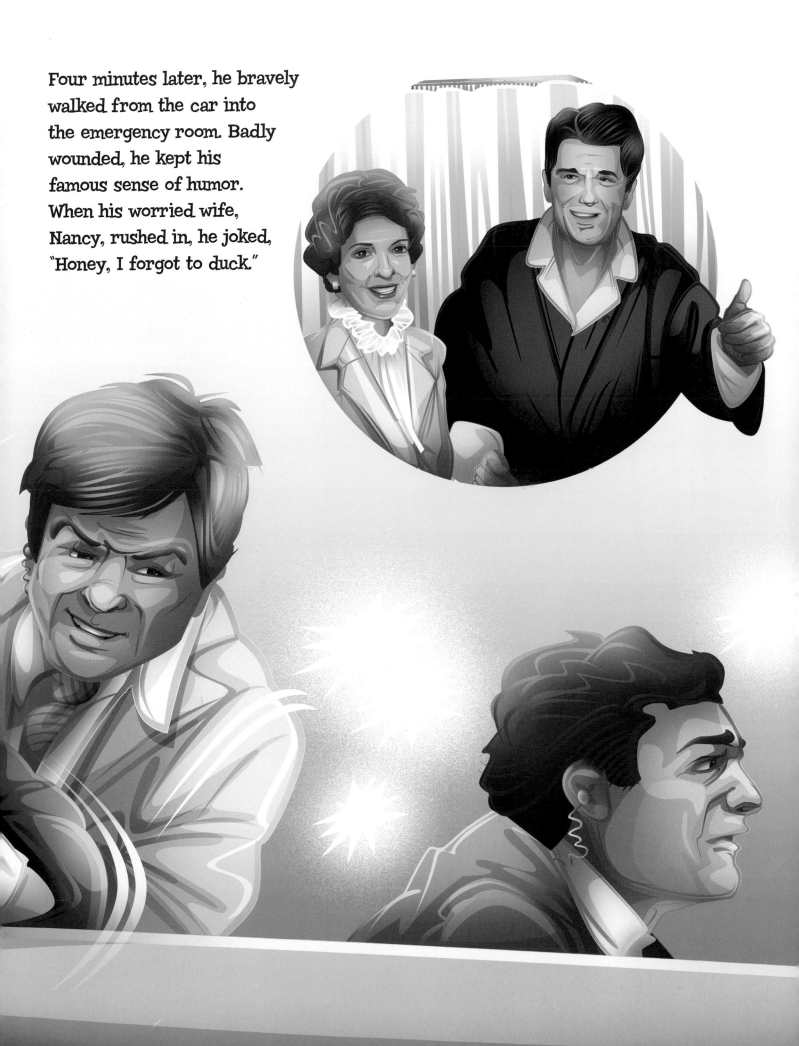

Four minutes later, he bravely walked from the car into the emergency room. Badly wounded, he kept his famous sense of humor. When his worried wife, Nancy, rushed in, he joked, "Honey, I forgot to duck."

President Reagan became known as the Great Communicator, because he always seemed to have the right words to say at the right time. He spoke often of America's greatness. In good times and bad, he spoke powerfully to unite the nation. Even in the very worst of times, like when the space shuttle *Challenger* exploded, he comforted the nation, telling them that the brave astronauts who died had "touched the face of God."

"Mr. Gorbachev, open this gate! Mr. Gorbachev, tear down this wall!" These were some of the most famous words President Reagan ever said. The Soviet Union was the most powerful communist nation, and Mikhail Gorbachev was its leader. Years before, East Germany's communist government built a wall right through the city of Berlin. On one side, the people were free. On the other side, they were not.

"Mr. Gorbachev, tear down this wall!"

Reagan believed that all people should be free, and he was brave enough to say so. Two years later, that wall came down. It was a huge step toward ending communism.

Reagan and Gorbachev later worked together and became such good friends that the president invited him to visit his favorite place on earth. At Rancho del Cielo, Reagan wore a white cowboy hat, and he gave his friend "Gorby" one too.

An invitation to the ranch was a special honor given to a select group of the Reagans' friends and family. Queen Elizabeth of Great Britain was another famous guest. Some came expecting a fancy mansion and were surprised to discover a simple adobe house and barn beside a pond.

Reagan described Rancho del Cielo as a magical place that makes you "feel as if you're on a cloud looking down at the world."

As Reagan prepared to leave office, he shared what he thought were the two best things that happened during his presidency. He was very proud that the American people had created millions of new jobs, but he was most proud that the world respected America again. He said, "We meant to change a nation, and instead, we changed a world."

Reagan started his life with big dreams. When he died in 2004 after a long illness, all his dreams (plus a whole lot more!) had come true in remarkable ways.

THE REMARKABLE RONALD REAGAN

Highlights from a Life Well-Lived

⭐ **February 6, 1911**
Ronald Wilson Reagan is born in Tampico, Illinois, to John (Jack) and Nelle Reagan.

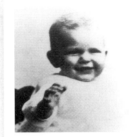

⭐ **1920**
After years of moving from town to town, the Reagan family settles in Dixon, Illinois.

⭐ **1924**
Reagan enters Dixon's Northside High School.

⭐ **1926**
Reagan spends the first of seven summers working as a lifeguard in Lowell Park on the Rock River.

⭐ **Fall 1928–Spring 1932**
Reagan attends Eureka College near Peoria, Illinois. Graduating with a dual degree in sociology and economics, he excelled as an actor, student leader, and football player.

⭐ **1932**
Within six weeks of graduation, Reagan begins his career as a radio sports announcer at WOC radio in Davenport, Iowa.

⭐ **April 29, 1937**
He enlists as a private in the Army Enlisted Reserve, and is assigned to serve with the 322nd Cavalry Regiment at Des Moines, Iowa.

⭐ **1937**
Reagan signs a seven-year acting contract with Warner Brothers.

⭐ **June 8, 1937**
He accepts an Officer's Commission and is appointed as a second lieutenant with the 323rd Cavalry Regiment in Los Angeles, California.

⭐ **January 26, 1940**
Reagan marries actress Jane Wyman.

⭐ **January 4, 1941**
Their daughter Maureen is born.

⭐ **April 19, 1942**
Reagan is ordered into active military duty following the Pearl Harbor attacks.

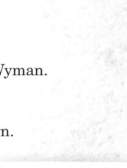

⭐ **March 1945**
Their son Michael is adopted.

⭐ **March 10, 1947**
Reagan is elected president of the Screen Actors Guild.

⭐ **June 6, 1948**
Reagan and Jane Wyman divorce.

⭐ **March 4, 1952**
He marries Nancy Davis.

THE REMARKABLE RONALD REAGAN

Highlights from a Life Well-Lived

⋆ **October 22, 1952**
Their daughter Patricia (Patti) is born.

⋆ **May 28, 1958**
Their son Ronald Prescott (Ron) is born.

⋆ **October 27, 1964**
Reagan delivers his "A Time for Choosing" speech on national television in support of Barry Goldwater for president and becomes known as a national political figure.

⋆ **January 1, 1966**
Reagan announces his candidacy for governor of California with promises to reduce the waste in government.

⋆ **November 8, 1966**
Reagan is elected by almost one million votes more than his opponent, incumbent Democratic governor Edmund G. ("Pat") Brown.

⋆ **January 3, 1967**
Reagan is sworn in as governor of California.

⋆ **August 5, 1968**
Reagan announces his candidacy for the presidential nomination but loses the primary to Richard Nixon.

⋆ **1970**
Reagan wins reelection as governor.

⋆ **January 18, 1973**
Reagan submits a $9.258 billion budget with a $1.1 billion surplus and gives taxpayers a rebate.

⋆ **November 13, 1974**
Ronald and Nancy Reagan purchase Rancho del Cielo.

⋆ **November 20, 1975**
Reagan runs for president again. This time he loses the primary race to the then current president Gerald Ford. Ford goes on to lose the election to Democrat Jimmy Carter.

⋆ **July 17, 1980**
Reagan accepts the Republican nomination for president.

⋆ **January 20, 1981**
Reagan is sworn in as the 40th president of the United States.

⋆ **March 30, 1981**
Reagan is shot by John Hinckley Jr. outside a Washington hotel. The bullet missed his heart by less than an inch, lodging in his lung and causing it to collapse.

⋆ **August 13, 1981**
He signs the Economic Recovery Tax Act at Rancho del Cielo.

⋆ **September 1981**
Reagan appoints the first female Supreme Court justice, Sandra Day O'Connor.

THE REMARKABLE RONALD REAGAN

Highlights from a Life Well-Lived

✸ **January 29, 1984**
Reagan formally announces he will seek reelection.

✸ **November 4, 1984**
Reagan defeats his Democratic opponent Walter Mondale in a landslide. Reagan carries 49 states—525 electoral votes to Mondale's 10, and 59 percent of the popular vote.

✸ **January 20, 1985**
Reagan is sworn in for a second term. At seventy-three years of age, he is the oldest president ever to take office.

✸ **January 28, 1986**
The U.S. space shuttle *Challenger* explodes only seventy-three seconds after takeoff. All six astronauts and the first civilian to go to space (teacher Christa McAuliffe) perish.

✸ **January 15, 1986**
Reagan signs legislation making the birthday of Martin Luther King Jr. a national holiday to be celebrated on the third Monday of January.

✸ **June 12, 1987**
Reagan challenges Soviet Leader Mikhail Gorbachev to tear down the Berlin Wall.

✸ **December 8, 1987**
Regan and Gorbachev sign the Intermediate-Range Nuclear Forces Treaty (INF Treaty)—a landmark agreement to eliminate an entire class of nuclear weapons.

✸ **January 14, 1989**
In his farewell address, Reagan states: "They called it the Reagan revolution. Well, I'll accept that, but for me it always seemed more like the great rediscovery, a rediscovery of our values and our common sense."

✸ **January 20, 1989**
George Bush is inaugurated; Ronald and Nancy Reagan fly to California. Reagan leaves office with the highest approval rating of any president since Franklin Roosevelt.

✸ **November 4, 1991**
The Reagan Library and Museum, located in Simi Valley, California, is dedicated.

✸ **1993**
Reagan is diagnosed with Alzheimer's disease.

✸ **November 5, 1994**
Reagan addresses a letter to the American people in which he discloses that he is suffering from Alzheimer's disease. He no longer appears in public.

✸ **June 5, 2004**
Ronald Reagan dies peacefully at his home in California. At age ninety-three, he lived longer than any president in American history.

Ronald Reagan: Pen Pals

President Reagan wrote more than ten thousand letters over his lifetime. Many, of course, were to important world leaders, many to beloved family and friends. Reagan especially enjoyed corresponding with children—both to hear their ideas and to encourage them.

Following are examples of some of the letters he sent and received from children:

President Reagan had an ongoing correspondence with a seven-year-old boy named Rudolph Lee-Hines. At the time Rudolph attended the Congress Heights Elementary School in Washington, D.C.; he received 175 letters from the president over a period of five years!

April 9, 1984
"You…mentioned reading and that is good. Rudolph, if you get in the habit of reading stories for pleasure you will never be lonely. Sometimes I worry that TV is going to rob young people of the great pleasure there is in a good book."

After President Reagan was shot, a second grader named Peter Sweeney from Riverside School in Rockville Centre sent the following note to the president:

"I hope you get well quick or you might have to make a speech in your pajamas.

P.S. If you have to make a speech in your pajamas, I warned you."

RONALD REAGAN

Feb. 15

Dear Sandy

Will you please tell your teacher and your classmates how very much I appreciate all their good wishes and kind thoughts. It is wonderful to know that young people like all of you with so much to keep you busy could still find time to hold out your hands in friendship to some one far away.

I hope you'll believe me when I say that my decision to enter the political race was because I want so much to help preserve this wonderful country for you and the Skipper and all young Americans. There are so many things to be thankful for in America, so many things that must not be lost; Our right to go to different churches; have our own ideas on government, choose our friends and what kind of work we'll do when we've finally finished our school days.

If some of us help keep this for you I know you'll keep it for other young people when you grow up. Again thanks

Ronald Reagan

Important Things Ronald Reagan Said

They called him the "Great Communicator" because somehow he always seemed to know just the right thing to say. Some of his most famous quotes were…

Sometimes Funny…

"I've often said there's nothing better for the inside of a man than the outside of a horse." (which he got from Winston Churchill)

"A hippie is someone who looks like Tarzan, walks like Jane, and smells like Cheetah."

"I have left orders to be awakened at any time in case of national emergency, even if I'm in a cabinet meeting."

"I hope you're all Republicans." (to surgeons as he entered the operating room following his assassination attempt)

"I want you to know I will not make age an issue of this campaign. I am not going to exploit, for political purposes, my opponent's youth and inexperience." (to Walter Mondale at a debate)

"But there are advantages to being elected president. The day after I was elected, I had my high school grades classified Top Secret."

"The nine most dangerous words in the English language are: I'm from the government and I'm here to help."

Sometimes Wise…

"Whatever else history may say about me when I'm gone, I hope it will record that I appealed to your best hopes, not your worst fears…."

"We can't help everyone, but everyone can help someone."

"The American dream is not that every man must be level with every other man. The American dream is that every man must be free to become whatever God intends he should become."

"We must reject the idea that every time a law's broken, society is guilty rather than the lawbreaker. It is time to restore the American precept that each individual is accountable for his actions."

Important Things Ronald Reagan Said

"All great change in America begins at the dinner table."

"I hope we have once again reminded people that man is not free unless government is limited. There's a clear cause and effect here that is as neat and predictable as a law of physics: as government expands, liberty contracts."

"Government's first duty is to protect the people, not run their lives."

"A people free to choose will always choose peace."

Sometimes Profound…

"You and I have a rendezvous with destiny. We will preserve for our children this, the last best hope of man on earth, or we will sentence them to take the first step into a thousand years of darkness. If we fail, at least let our children and our children's children say of us we justified our brief moment here. We did all that could be done."

"Freedom is never more than one generation away from extinction."

"If we lose freedom here, there is no place to escape to. This is the last stand on earth."

"Let us resolve tonight that young Americans will always…find there a city of hope in a country that is free. And let us resolve they will say of our day and our generation that we did keep the faith with our God, that we did act 'worthy of ourselves,' that we did protect and pass on lovingly that shining city on a hill."

For More Information:

To find out more about the Rancho del Cielo, go online to http://www.yaf.org/TheReaganRanch.aspx.

To find out more about the life and times of Ronald Reagan, go online to the Ronald Reagan Foundation and Library at http://www.reaganfoundation.org.

There is no limit to what a man
can do or where he can go if he doesn't mind
who gets the credit.

—Words of wisdom from Ronald Reagan